Alex Khayutin

THE BALLAD OF
BLOOD AND POWER

A rhymed English-Russian bilingual tale

The creations in this volume belong to:

"Memoria Cordis media"

c/o Alex Khayutin, Hamilton, Canada

Copyright © by Alex Khayutin

All rights reserved.

Canadian International Standard Book Number (ISBN):
978-1-0688661-8-0

Introduction

From the infamous assassination of Julius Caesar to the present day, history has long been shaped by political murders. These fatal events fascinate scholars and authors alike, who study how they alter the fates of individuals and entire nations.

Imperial Russia was no exception, witnessing its share of bloody assassinations. Emperor Paul I was murdered in his bedchamber in 1801 by a group of disgruntled military nobles. In 1882, Emperor Alexander II fell to an assassin from an early clandestine revolutionary cell. Prime Minister Pyotr Stolypin, despised by many during Tsar Nicholas II's reign, was shot in 1908 before hundreds of eyewitnesses while attending a theater performance in Kyiv.

The most well-known political assassination of the early Bolshevik regime was the attempt on Vladimir

Lenin's life in August 1918. His would-be assassin, Fanny Kaplan, a political opponent, gravely wounded him. Lenin survived and ruled for another six years, but Kaplan's execution marked the beginning of the Red Terror. Other Bolshevik leaders, such as Moisey Uritsky and V. Volodarsky, were also assassinated in the chaotic years following the October Revolution. Even Leon Trotsky, one of the revolution's key figures, was murdered in exile in 1940 by a Stalinist agent.

The infamous show trials of the 1930s saw many prominent Bolsheviks executed under false accusations, reinforcing Stalin's growing cult of personality. Amid this dark period, one of the most tragic political assassinations in Soviet history occurred on December 1, 1934—the murder of Sergei Kirov, First Secretary of the Leningrad Communist Party Organization. His death, like a bolt from the blue, shook the entire country.

A trusted friend and close confidant of Stalin, Kirov had once been a tireless enforcer of the Party line. By the late 1920s and early 1930s, however, he had risen as a beloved leader of the rapidly industrializing Soviet Russia. Respected by Party members at all levels, Kirov's influence grew—perhaps too much for Stalin's comfort. Some of Kirov's views clashed with Stalin's, particularly regarding the harsh treatment of Party personnel. At the 1932 Party Plenum, Kirov even received more votes than Stalin in a secret ballot for the membership in the Communist Party's Central Committee. Kirov was a powerful, charismatic speaker and a very popular figure both within the party and generally. It is no stretch to imagine that Stalin could see him as a threat to his own leadership role.

Kirov's assassin, Leonid Nikolayev, allegedly held a personal grudge—enraged that Kirov was romantically involved with his former wife, who worked as Kirov's secretary. Presumably, he also decided to take revenge on Kirov after he was thrown out of the party for "breaching party discipline," and could no longer get food rations available to party apparatchiks. Arrested immediately after murdering Kirov, Nikolayev was swiftly interrogated, including by Stalin himself, convicted, and executed.

Though no definitive archival verification links Stalin directly to the murder, many historians argue that circumstantial evidence suggests his involvement. At the time, Kirov, an ethnic Russian, was seen—especially by veteran Party members—as a more amiable alternative to Stalin, whose reputation for cruelty and sharpness toward colleagues was well known.

The bilingual rhymed tale presented here, was originally written in Russian and translated into English by the author. It dramatizes the fateful encounter between Kirov and Stalin, set on the brink of Kirov's murder. The encounter imagines a political clash between the two, that seals Kirov's tragic fate.

While rooted in historical facts, this account remains a work of fiction.

Real figures—Stalin, Kirov, Yagoda—and historical events such as kulak repression and NKVD purges seek to ground the story in the grim reality of Stalinist rule. Introducing a mysterious middleman between the Kremlin and the assassin, the narrative tries to build a sense of dread and inevitability. Stalin is not merely a ruler here, but a calculating, conscience-free manipulator. His enforcer, Yagoda, carries out his blood-stained will. Kirov is shown as the one who speaks the truth, but his honesty seals his fate.

This historical narrative tries not only to keep Stalin's menace palpable, but also attempts to be a reflection on power, fear and conspiracy - where absolute authority demands absolute loyalty, with those who challenge it paying the ultimate price.

Kirov Speaking at the 17th Party Congress, 1934

"The Ballad of Blood and Power"

They killed Kirov[1]!

Murdered him!

How diligently we forgot

About this dirty secret!

That deadly shot on the hasty December Day

Thrown on all, madly,

Clamping painful shouts in our breasts,

Stalin, yanking the Smolny hall up,

Shoving his fist into Russia's face,

---

[1] *Kirov, Sergei – 27.03.1886 – 01.12. 1934 – Russian Bolshevik revolutionary, member of the Party Politburo, friend of Stalin*

I want to turn this nastiness
Inside out…

…Braking dark covers,
I look into the Kremlin windows...

***

"Well, Myronych[2], why are you silent?"
Stalin moved his black eyebrow,
"We shall show kulaks[3] a fist,
And wipe out this kulak avalanche!

---

[2] *Myronych – short for Mironovich, patronymic of Kirov*

[3] *Kulak – wealthy independent farmer*

The deprived are betting on us,

And we are aware of their alarm,

Kulaks are common enemies! As a class!

So, let's move them all into Siberian Den!"

"My heart is pained as if by a huge cut

When I hear that rumble,

These groans gnashing across Volga-River!"

And Kirov stretched his hand

Towards a window:

"What an unlucky nation

To be molded and refolded!

Today - pulled to the left,

Tomorrow - to the right,

Today – marching to a war,

Tomorrow - to a parade!

Today – an increased producer's quota,

Tomorrow – a new tax,

Then – the NEP[4]!

Listen, really

They are more than right

Trashing such authorities!

I am afraid, that somewhere we've

Committed so many absurd mistakes

They'd be right in removing us!

Take kulaks for instance:

Instead of squeezing them out

We simply started killing them!

Cattle farms in villages are half naked,

It's cows seized to collective farms,

Where they have newspapers for forage

In a mix with hungry diarrhea!

---

[4] *NEP – acronym for the New Economic Policy*

And peasants are right spitting
Into eyes of such a worker's party
…So, I shall not vote "for"
At the upcoming party meeting,
Much as it makes you unhappy!

People stopped trusting us,
The very same people that feed
You and me.
And even though you are a "great Stalin",
You still don't know how to milk cows!"

He faltered, looking gloomily,
Said:
"Sorry – my bad temper!
But even a proletarian dictatorship
Must not rash its actions!"

As though bitterness of "Kazbek" tobacco
Had warped his lips,
But Stalin quickly overcame it:
"Wow, what is it with you?

Yes, I know, there were excesses,
Let's state and get rid of them!
But you better tell me how we could
Force them to understand us?

We need to feed the army, the workers,
Where all the kulaks ever want
Is to snatch more from us!
A very few among them keen
To even selling us bread or meat,

And even those few who do,
Try hard to rip us off.
And you are saying to me "leave them
Alone?"
When they will eat us raw if we do!

The Soviet power is not worth
Two pence
If workers are starving,
And if we are unable to hack this
Adversity,

Then, yes, it's time to remove us!

Let's not get excited,

I am not deaf – I hear these groans!

But today whoever powers over wheat

Has the control over the country!

Yes! Over the entire country!

And there are no other recipes,

And future historians will forgive us

For our methods»,

Added doggedly:

"You chop wood – you get woodchips

Flying!"

"But you, my friend",

Kirov turned to pick up an overcoat,

"Can trust me

That if Lenin were still alive,

He would strip for that of the

Party Membership"

"Why is it all of you
Keep on yapping to me – Lenin, Lenin?"
Stalin's chickenpox face rushes,
"The nation is swamped up to its knees,
But you, as the pack of these political
Rascals,
Whom we have just stopped,
Are sticking to the fantasy of internal
Freedom,
To these Lenin's teachings!

I am telling you - no, we are not going to
Wait for years,
Until these country folk
Would pick at our kolkhoz[5] with their
Curious noses,

---

[5] *Kolkhoz – acronym for a collective farm*

Later gossiping quietly,

About its merits or negatives!"

His hand slicing pressing air,

Stalin once again put his pipe in a mouth:

"It's late Mironych, go!

Let's argue about "your people"

Tomorrow!"

But Kirov hesitates, visibly,

Stern face clearing,

Says quietly but very distinctly:

"Soso[6], I....I really did not want to...

---

[6] *Koba, Soso - Stalin's nicknames used by the close friends*

Forgive me, but...
Something is Happening...
Something is wrong with the Party...
Whoever keeps on finding new enemies
May end up being an enemy himself!

Recall those we'd labelled
"Opportunists"?
Accused – may be in a useless rage?
All – flesh and blood communists!
Most – Lenin's confidants!

He valued them, whereas we expelled
These people he'd trusted!
Could it be that it's me, or even you,
Who are unfair and biased?

Having rejected Lenin's advice,
We are forcing into our collective farms,
And if you are serious about it,
Ask yourself: who is really biased here?"

Very quietly, hardly audibly,

Without looking at Stalin:

"I am only baffled by one thing,

How seeing it all,

I could still vote "for"?"

And left….

Stalin has lowered his body

Gauging an armchair,

And suddenly…quickly crossed himself,

Smoked pipe full of devilish fire

Flashing in a lunar twilight

Of a room filled with darkness.

"Me? To be removed? What utter nonsense!"

And he pressed the call button.

Kirov, how impossibly direct were you!

You rose almost to His level,

But instead of being obedient

You threatened to step onto that pedestal,

On which there was enough space
Only for one!
For one leader only - Him!
For all of Russia – only him, Stalin,
As God, as their supreme master!

"Bring in Yagoda[7] at midnight!"
Stalin orders,
"Where's Kirov?
Bound for Leningrad
On the Red Arrow train,
Was on time to get on it?"
He nodded, pretending to be pleased...

***

---

[7] *Yagoda, Genrikh – Minister of the State Security at the time*

Kirov and Stalin on Vacation in Sochi

Stalin – this defective shard of being,
He was not poured out of steel
Instead, he was poured out of
Continuous human grief,
That he'd generated
Around himself.

The flesh and blood of ultimate power,
He always accepted
It's cardinal rule:
The closer one was to the "throne",
The more threatening one grew.

Within the boundaries of his
Domain,
Of the one sixth
Of the Earth,
He'd transformed people in thirty years

Into what the Tartars could not achieve

In three hundred[8].

It pains

To look at these bleak faces,

Of almost identical expressions,

Surrounded by the

Buttonholed guards

Shielding this ring of

Hopelessness.

No - there does not exist a vicious

Circle of evil,

Just a stamp of indifference!

Just a gene of congenital

---

[8] *Reference to the so called (Mongol) Tartar Yoke that Russia had suffered from about 1230th to the end of the 15th Century*

Fright,

Telling all to be silent:

Always! Everywhere!

Rooted by their nature into

Grasping at pitchforks or axes

At a slightest tip-off,

Today – there is silence

In people,

And not by bayonets, not

Because of fences,

But just simply because: "the Party said So",

And, as if everyone had lost their minds!

Everyone: from Leningrad to Baikal,

In Ryazan, Irkutsk,

And Bugulma…!

I hear the voices

Reaching me from that mausoleum:

"Clamp the throat of that Jew!"

... That line, that state border line –

Which I crossed – it is left in the past,

A border of that country,

Where my mother gave birth to me,

Where I did not have to be born,

But still was,

And yes, I should bow for that…

Terrified that

I have taken away with me not only

Memory,

And shame from bent

Knees,

But may be that gene of fright

It was hiding in my luggage as well?

I know I was smacked by verbal abuse

And the lead

Of the sailors from that battleship - "Aurora"[9],
Stalin – as if the public prosecutor
Staring into my face,

Maybe it was not exactly me –
Maybe it was my father's face,
Don't have to be specific.
After all,
We were all exemplary,
In knowing how to keep silent!

---

[9] *Battleship "Aurora" - the gunshot from the "Aurora" sent the signal to storm the Winter Palace during the Russian Bolshevik Revolution.*

"Comrade" Stalin taught us
That sons do not answer for
Their fathers' deeds!
Iron-clad formulas
Shining in speeches
Of the evil man,

If I do not have to answer -
Then who does?

Every last one of us - the children
Of his system!

***

A real enigma for all, however,
Are the Russians such as Yagoda!

***

Perhaps in a very distant future,
Once our souls split into atoms,
You would put out in writing thick
Volumes,

Filled with the full understanding of man,

Where in computer codes

Of a simple and eternal catalogue,

There would be place for everyone:

Where first freedom fighters

Would be next to conquered nations,

And incorrigible drunks – next to eternal God!

I know that the words

"Distant exile" won't exist

In your future dictionaries,

And when your mothers would kiss their

Sons,

They won't think about prisons

And concentration camps.

I wish I woke up under your arches,

I wish I smiled and shook your hands,

As I want to forget about Genrikh Yagoda,

And wish I could ever stop thinking

About my martyred mother!

They were all swearing

In the name of the Danko's heart[10],

In the name of the heart – torch!

That heart – they turned it into a lie!

This crazy youth –

They carried only troubles

In their horse drawn "tachankas"[11]

Later, they would shoot happily

Into the Gulag crowds,

Manufacture false convictions,

Danko's torch burning down

---

[10] *Danko's heart – Danko is a character from the Russian writer Maxim Gorky's story "Old Woman Izergil", who sacrificed himself and saved his people with the help of a burning heart.*

[11] *Tachanka – a horse drown machine gun cart or wagon*

Groaning bodies of the innocent!

Sword-belted NKVD[12]-shnik

Seating at every table….

…The country waiting, reverently,

For Genrikh's arrival...

***

... He walked in quickly, without a report,

Froze, breathing slowly,

Without taking his gaze

From the red pencil,

---

[12] *NKVD – an acronym for the People Commissariat for Internal Affairs*

From the hands that flipped

A stack of folded papers.

"Sit down!", said Stalin disdainfully,

Thinking: "that fool will do it!"

***

Oh, how he despised

All these souls,

All of them like

Spiders in a glass jar.

Like shameless, obedient

Herd,

Selling for a handful

Of loose change,

Or anything else

Their past dreams,

Past ideals,

Who, like greenhorns

Were boasting about

Being somebody,

Being someone,

Being ready for anything -

Devoted to him, Stalin,

To the bone,

Hooray!

Just leave them their cozy

Nooks.

***

Yagoda was stained with blood
Not by his elbows – but all over!
How else would his personal file
Read: "diligent and dutiful".

…He tore a page from a notebook,
Swallowed pipe smoke
Brushing away drops of sweat
Into a hidden handkerchief.

But Stalin, with a half-squinted glance,
Tightening last psycho-screw,
Uttered: "Hide your notebook,
Today, you don't have to write!

There is a hidden treachery
Among remnants of undefeated enemy,
NKVD protecting our state,
With a sword in a punishing hand.

With the sword, Yagoda, not with a
Notebook,
I want to see the ranks of
Internal Affairs!

Tomorrow, take the early flight
To Leningrad,
Stop at the doctor's office
Down the hall, after we finish,
The door is to the left,
Take the cadaveric poison from him,
Don't be afraid,

It's in the form of a bread loaf,

And with that - straight to Leningrad!

You, Commissar,

Have rich experience:

Chayanov and Shakhty Trials,

Chernow and Trotskyists[13]

Impudent diggings,

You told us all about them,

But this, this!

---

[13] *Chayanov trial, Shakhty trial, Chernov trial, Trotskyists' trials – public trials carried out by Stalin's satraps against various groups of those opposed to Stalin's plans for industrialization of Russia.*

Such is the character, the nature

Of our enemy,

Such is the cunning,

That if they can't find support

Among people,

They will resolve to terror!

In the quarters of the Northern Capital,

Where the unfinished scum howls,

People are facing the rising hand

Of A Mercenary Assassin.

And you will find that hand

And

... place the dagger into it!"

Added Stalin,

And quietly stood up.

Yagoda began to tremble,

Wanting to kneel down

His hair - on end under the shirt,

Lenin looking from the wall picture,

Knowingly: he was nothing,

And Stalin was everything.

Turning white and slurring,

Not wanting to admit, but realizing

At once, *"WHO"*,

He barely exhaled: "I see!"

"Put on a civilian coat,

And upon arrival

Run to the Vitebsk train station,

Buy a seat on the express train,

I personally reserved at the cashier's

Window,

To Lithuania.

Find an excuse

To put the bag with the bread

In that person's luggage

And use the government wire

To report to me personally, when done!

Any questions?"

Still clinging to hope,

Yagoda blurted:

"For how long am I to Lithuania?"

Stalin got angry:

"You fool!"

Such commissars as you

Are only good as farm hands!

Even Menzhinsky[14] was probably
Smarter,
If only he did not remember that
Lenin's Hut!
A ticket to Lithuania – for the one, who
Will find the Assassin,
And bread - for his hand luggage!
But where, of what color,
Or who this beast lives with -
That's Yagoda for you to answer!"

And Stalin stepped out the door ...

***

---

[14] *Menzhinsky, Vyacheslav – a Soviet revolutionary and politician, served as a Chairman of the secret police of the Soviet Union.*

Poor boy from Urzhum[15],
Your clock was already ticking,
And around the corner, silently
Your death was smiling into a mustache.

And at the hour of the bloody signal,
The innocent would clog the jail cameras,
Shot at point blank!

The moment when Kirov died,
The real Stalinist terror was born.

A bullet saved for Yagoda,
Was used on him before sunset,
Him - the last among those who knew ...

---

[15] *Urzhum – a city, the birth place of Kirov*

... Soldiers found the corpse in a boxcar,
When the express train from Leningrad
Arrived to the Wilno Station.

...The man was dark-haired,
His blood blackened by the
Cadaveric venom.
...He was never identified by the senior
Border guards...

Stalin next to Kirov coffin, December 1934

A Few Biographical Notes About Sergei Kirov

- **Born** on March 26, 1886, in Urzhum, Russia, one of seven children.
- **Orphaned** at the age of seven in 1893; raised by his paternal grandmother, then placed in an orphanage.
- **In 1901**, a group of wealthy benefactors provided Kirov with a scholarship to attend an industrial school, where he earned a degree in engineering.
- **In 1904**, while working in Tomsk, Siberia, Kirov joined the Russian Social Democratic Workers' Party.
- **1905–1917:** Lived in the Caucasus, participating in revolutionary activities.
- **1917–1920:** Took part in the Russian Civil War on the Bolshevik side; became commander of the Astrakhan Military Administration.
- **In 1921**, Kirov was appointed First Secretary of the Communist Party of the Azerbaijan Soviet Socialist Republic.
- **In 1926**, he became First Secretary of the Leningrad District of the All-Union Communist Party (Bolsheviks).
- **On December 1, 1934,** Kirov was assassinated by Leonid Nikolaev. His remains were cremated,

and his ashes were interred in the Kremlin Wall Necropolis with the highest state honors.

Russian Language Original.

БАЛАДА О КРОВИ И ВЛАСТИ

Убили Кирова! Убили!
Как все старательно забыли
Об этой тайне грязной мы!

Декабрь рванулся из зимы
На резкий выстрел страшно, шало,
И болью крик в груди зажало.
Так Сталин, вздыбив Смольный зал,
Кулак России показал.

Хочу я вывернуть нутро
У этой подлости наружу,
Покровы темные нарушив,
Смотрю в кремлевское окно.

***

- «Ну, что-ж Мироныч ты молчишь?»
И Сталин черной бровью двинул,
- «Мы кулаку покажем шиш,
Сметем кулацкую лавину!

Бедняк надеется на нас,
И нам близка его тревога,
Наш враг – кулачество! Как класс!
Так всех – в сибирскую берлогу!»

- «Огромной болью сердце режет,
Когда я слышу этот гул,
Какой по Волге стон и скрежет!»
И Киров руку протянул
К окну.

- «Несчастная держава!
В который раз в ней все кроят!
То влево дергают, то – вправо,
То – на войну, то – на парад!

То – продразверсткой, то – налогом,

То – НЭПом! Слушай, ей-богу

Ведь правы, коль такую власть

Обложат матюгами всласть!

Боюсь, что где-то наломали

Мы с этим – впору нас снимать!

Вот кулаков, не вытесняли,

А просто стали убивать!

Дворы в деревнях пораздеты,

Коровы согнаны в колхоз,

А там на корм – одни газеты,

Голодный, кровяной понос!

И нам-же, партии рабочих,

Крестьяне наплюют в глаза.

Нет, я на пленуме, как хочешь,

Голосовать не буду «за»!

Нам люди верить перестали,

А им ведь нас с тобой кормить,

И ты, хоть и «великий Сталин»,

Не знаешь, как коров доить!»

Запнулся, тут-же глянул хмуро,

Сказал:

- «Прости, я – сгоряча!

Но мы, хотя и диктатура,

Не смеем их рубить с плеча!»

Как будто горечью «Казбека»

Перекосило губы вкруг,

Но Сталин поборол их:

- «Эка! Ты что это, Мироныч, вдруг?

Да, знаю, были перегибы,

Укажем, будут устранять!

Скажи-ка лучше, как могли мы

Заставить их себя понять?

Нам армию кормить, рабочих,

А кулаку – свое урвать!

А сколько было их, охочих,

Нам хлеб и мясо продавать?

На всю округу если, двое,

И те обвесить норовят,

А ты – «оставить их в покое!»

Да нас – утопят! Нас – съедят!

И грош цена советской власти,

Коли рабочим голодать,

Ну, а не справимся с напастью,

Что-ж, верно, впору нас снимать!

Давай не будем горячиться,

Я слышу стоны – не глухой!

Но у кого в руках пшеница,

Тот управляет все страной!

Да всей! И нет других рецептов,
И нас историки простят
За методы»,
И глянул цепко:
- «Лес рубишь – щепочки летят!»

- «А Ленин, будь он жив, за это
Лишил-бы, к черту, партбилета,
Уж ты по-дружески поверь!»
И Киров взялся за шинель.

- «Да что вы все мне – Ленин, Ленин?»
Рванулся оспенным лицом,
- «Страна увязла по колени,
А ты, как кучка подлецов,

Которым мы не дали ходу,
Мне тычешь мнимую свободу,
Да этот ленинский завет!
Нет, мы не будем ждать сто лет,
Пока крестьянские умишки
К нам сунут любопытный нос,

Чтобы потом судачить тишком,
А что - колхоз, да как – колхоз!»

И, резанув давящий воздух,
Он трубку снова сунул в рот.
- «Иди, Мироныч, очень поздно!
Поспорим завтра «за народ!»

Но Киров медлил, непонятно,
И строгий взгляд его яснел,
Затем негромко, очень внятно:
- «Сосо, я очень не хотел...

Прости, но...что-то происходит...
И что-то в партии – не так!
...Кто каждый день врагов находит,
Сам может оказаться... враг!

Ты вспомни, кто – в «оппортунистах»?
И обвинен – не сгоряча-ль?
Все – плоть от плоти – коммунисты!
Все – окруженье Ильича!

Он их ценил, а мы – изгнали
Людей, которым верил он!
А может - Киров, может – Сталин,
Сегодня в партии уклон?

Отбросив Ленина советы,
Мы, силой, гоним в наш колхоз,
Всерьез подумаешь об этом,
Кто уклонист – еще вопрос?»

И очень тихо, чуть невнятно,
Не глядя Сталину в глаза:
- «Одно мне только непонятно,
Как мог я высказаться «за»?

И вышел.

Сталин опустился
Наощупь в кресло, замер в нем,
И вдруг...со лба перекрестился,
И трубка, бесовским огнем,

Блеснула в лунном полумраке,
Он свет еще не зажигал.
«Меня? Снимать? Не дамся! Враки!»
И кнопку вызова нажал.

Эх, Киров, как ты прямодушен!
Когда почти-что вровень встал,
Так нет того, чтобы послушен!
Шагнуть грозишь на пьедестал.

Но место есть на пьедестале – одно!
И вождь, для всех – один!
На всю Россию – только Сталин,
Как Бог, как высший господин!

- «На полночь вызови Ягоду!
Что Киров? Отбыл в Ленинград?
Прямой «Стрелой»? Успел к отходу?»
Он сделал вид, что очень рад...

***

Был не из стали
Вылит Сталин,
Ущербный сколок
Бытия,
А из сплошной
Людской печали,
Что породил
Вокруг себя.

И ставши, плоть от плоти –
Властью,
Всегда ценил
Ее закон:
Чем ближе к трону –
Тем опасней,
И тем заманчивее
Трон!

В границах своего

Надела,

В одну шестую часть

Земли,

Он, в тридцать лет,

С народом сделал,

Татары – в триста

Не смогли!

Мне – боль

Смотреть на эти

Лица,

Все – будто на одно

Лицо!

На окружение

В петлицах,

На безысходности

Кольцо.

Нет заколдованного
Круга,
Есть – безразличия
Печать!
Есть – ген врожденного
Испуга,
Всегда, везде, на все –
Молчать!

По корневой своей
Природе,
Чуть-что -
За вилы и топор,
Сегодня – тишина
В народе!
И не штыки, и не
Забор,
А просто: «Партия сказала»,
И, будто, все сошли
С ума!
От Ленинграда до Байкала,

Рязань, Иркутск,
И Бугульма!

Сюда, с трибуны
Мавзолея,
Мне долетают
Голоса:
"Заткните глотку у
еврея!"

...Осталась в прошлом
Полоса,
Черта, рубежная
Граница,
Страна, где матерью
Рожден,
Где мог бы, вовсе,
Не родиться,
Ну, что-же,
И на том, поклон!

Но я увез не только
Память,
И стыд от согнутых
Колен,
А вдруг, в моем багажном
Хламе,
Сидел того испуга
Ген?

По мне ударила
«Аврора»
Матросской бранью и
Свинцом,
И Сталин, взглядом
Прокурора,
В мое уставился
Лицо.

Ну, не в мое, пускай,
В отцово,
Что за резоны
Уточнять?

Мы все умели,
Образцово,
На то, что нужно,
Промолчать!

Нас научил товарищ
Сталин:
Сын – не в ответе за
Отца!
Стальные формулы
Блистали,
В речах злодея-
Мудреца.

Я – не в ответе!
Кто – в ответе?
Мы все – его системы
Дети!

***

Загадка русского народа,

Такие люди, как Ягода!

***

Быть может вы, в далекой дали,

На атом души расщепя,

Тома толстенные издали,

С познанием самих себя.

В компьютерические коды,

В простой и вечный каталог,

Вошли и «первенцы свободы»,

И покоренные народы,

И вечный пьяница, и Бог!

Нет слова этого, «чужбина»,

Я знаю, в ваших словарях,

И мать, когда целует сына,

Не думает о лагерях.

Я к вам хочу, под ваши своды,
С улыбкой руки пожимать,
Забыть про Генриха Ягоду,
Забыть замученную мать!

Они клялись про сердце Данко,
Про сердце – факел! Сердце – ложь!
Везла беду в своих тачанках,
Шальная эта молодежь.

Ну а потом, стреляла в «зону»,
«Лепила» ложные дела,
И факел Данко жег до стона,
Невинных черные тела!
Энкавэдэшник портупейно
Засел у каждого стола,
Страна ждала, благоговейно,
Прихода Генриха ждала!

***

...Вошел он быстро, без доклада,
У двери замер, чуть дыша,
Не отрывая впертость взгляда
От красного карандаша,

От рук, которые листали
Стопу из сложенных бумаг.
- «Садитесь!» молвил властно Сталин,
Подумал: «выполнит, дурак!»

***

Как презирал он
Эти души,
Всех этих, в банке,
Пауков,
Кто стыдно, стадно
Был послушен,
Продав за горстку
Пятаков,
Или еще какого
Блага,

Идею, преданность

Мечте,

Кто, как зеленейший

«Салага»,

Еще бахвалился

Меж тем,

Что он-де, что-то,

Он-де, кто-то,

Что предан –

До седьмого пота!

Что он готов на все -

Ура!

Но, чур, за ним его

Нора!

***

Ягода кровью был запачкан,

Куда по локти? С головой!

Откуда-бы ему, иначе

Иметь в анкете, «деловой»?

Он вырвал листик из блокнота,

Глотая трубочный дымок,
Смахнул платком росинки пота,
И спрятал носовой платок.

А Сталин, в пол прищура взглядом,
Последний психодоворот:
«Сегодня, вам писать не надо,
Сегодня, спрячьте ваш блокнот!

Есть потаенное коварство
У недобитого врага.
ЧеКа – защита государства,
С мечом в карающих руках.

С мечом, Ягода, не с блокнотом,
Я видеть органы хочу!
Назавтра, первым самолетом
Летите в Питер,

Ко врачу,
По коридору, дверь налево,
Зайдя, возьмете трупный яд,
Не бойтесь, это – в виде хлеба,

И с этим, прямо в Ленинград!
У вас, нарком, богатый опыт:
Чаянов, «шахтинцы», Чернов,
Троцкистов наглые подкопы
Вы нам раскрыли, но таков

Характер, такова природа:
Идейный враг – куда хитер,
Коль нет поддержки у народа,
Они пойдут и на террор!

В кварталах северной столицы,
Где, недобито, воет мразь,
Рука наемного убийцы
В лицо народа поднялась.

И вы найдете эту руку
Чтобы...
...Вложить в нее кинжал!»
Добавил Сталин, встал без стука,
Ягода мелко задрожал,

Хотел валиться на колени,

Под майкой - дыбом волосье,

Взирал на них портретно Ленин,

Он был – ничто, а Сталин – все.

И побелело, и невнятно,

Еще не зная, понял «КТО»,

Ответил-выдохнул: «Понятно!»

- «Наденьте штатское пальто,

И по прибытии на место,

Бегом, на Витебский вокзал,

Возьмете место на курьерский,

Я, лично, в кассе заказал

Билет в Литву.

Найдете повод

В багаж засунуть ваш пакет,

И, взяв правительственный провод,

Мне доложить! Вопросов нет?»

Еще цепляясь за надежду,
Спросил:
- «Насколько я, в Литву?»
Озлился Сталин,
- «Ты, невежда!
Таких наркомов – на ботву!

Менжинский был умней, пожалуй,
Жаль, помнил ленинский шалаш!
Билет в Литву – тому, с кинжалом,
И хлеб – в его ручной багаж!

А кто он, где, какого цвета,
С кем обитает этот зверь –
Тебе, Ягода, для ответа!»
И Сталин тихо вышел в дверь...

**

Несчастный мальчик из Уржума,
Еще идут, стучат часы,
Но за углом твоим, бесшумно,
Смерть улыбается в усы.

Чтоб в час кровавого сигнала,
Забить подвалы, и – в упор!
В тот миг, как Кирова не стало,
Родился сталинский террор.

Ягоде – пулю пред закатом,
Последнему из тех, кто знал...

...В вагоне труп нашли солдаты,
Когда на вильнюсский вокзал,
Пришел экспресс из Ленинграда.

...Мужчина был черноволос,
Чернел анализ трупным ядом,
Но кто он, старшему наряда
Установить не удалось...

www.ingramcontent.com/pod-product-compliance
Lightning Source LLC
Chambersburg PA
CBHW042300030526
44119CB00066B/838